· ICE CREAM ·

the perfect weekend treat

· ICE CREAM ·

the perfect weekend treat

Susanna Tee

Marks and Spencer p.l.c.
Baker Street, London, W1U 8EP
www.marksandspencer.com

Produced by The Bridgewater Book Company Ltd

Photographer Calvey Taylor-Haw
Home Economist Ruth Pollock

ISBN 1-84461-083-7
Printed in China

Notes for the reader
- This book uses both metric and imperial measurements. Follow the same units of measurement throughout; do not mix metric and imperial.
- All spoon measurements are level: teaspoons are assumed to be 5 ml, and tablespoons are assumed to be 15 ml.
- Unless otherwise stated, eggs are assumed to be medium.
- Recipes using raw eggs should be avoided by infants, the elderly, pregnant women, convalescents and anyone suffering from an illness.

contents

introduction

Few of us can resist licking an ice cream in a cone on a hot summer's day, spooning into a rich, creamy ice cream for dessert or savouring a smooth, cold sorbet after a good meal. Ice cream is probably one of the most popular desserts of all. It is a firm favourite with children and a cool, refreshing choice for adults.

Making your own ice cream or sorbet at home is a surprisingly simple process. If you are lucky enough to own an ice cream machine, then there is very little effort and time involved. A machine is not essential, however, and you can make successful ice creams without one using the traditional method of beating the ice cream mixture during freezing. The recipes in this book give instructions for making ice creams and sorbets by either method.

Commercial ice cream can be good but nothing can compare to a home-made variety where you know exactly what ingredients have been used. Rich ice creams, sorbets and iced desserts can all be found in this collection of recipes. There's no substitute for the real thing, however wicked it may be, so on that note, enjoy!

There's no substitute for the real thing

coolest ic

coolest
ice creams

Who can resist a cool, smooth, indulgent ice cream? The secret of making a smooth ice cream is to beat the mixture in order to break down the ice crystals. An ice cream machine will do this for you but, made in a freezer, the crystals can easily be beaten halfway through freezing. A food processor efficiently beats the mixture in a matter of moments, although you can also do the beating by hand. The recipes here require you to beat once during freezing but, if you have time, a second beating would not go amiss.

Ice creams taste best if they are not eaten too cold, so take them out of the freezer a short time before serving. Between 15 and 30 minutes is about the right length of time. This also allows the ice cream to soften slightly, which makes it easier to scoop and serve. Alternatively, if you really can't wait, pop the ice cream into the microwave in bursts of 30 seconds until it has softened.

When it comes to serving ice creams, crisp, thin, sweet biscuits are the perfect partner for them, so keep a selection of interesting biscuits in your store cupboard to serve at a moment's notice. A stack of cones could be useful too, especially if there are children around. Meringues also make a good accompaniment: a batch of them could easily be whisked up using those left-over egg whites.

The recipes in this chapter are collected from around the world and include a classic Rich Vanilla Ice Cream, an aromatic Indian Kulfi and a colourful Italian Pistachio Gelato. They are truly cool!

e creams

The praline in this recipe has been made with almonds, but blanched hazelnuts, which are the other nuts that praline is traditionally made with, macadamias or pine kernels are equally good.

Chocolate Praline Ice Cream

INGREDIENTS

85 g/3 oz plain dark chocolate, broken into pieces
300 ml/10 fl oz full-fat milk
85 g/3 oz caster sugar
3 egg yolks
300 ml/10 fl oz whipping cream
PRALINE
vegetable oil, for oiling
100 g/3½ oz granulated sugar
2 tbsp water
50 g/1¾ oz blanched almonds

SERVES 4–6

To prepare the praline, brush a baking tray with oil. Put the sugar, water and nuts in a large heavy-based saucepan and heat gently, stirring, until the sugar has dissolved, then let the mixture bubble gently for 6–10 minutes, or until lightly golden brown. Do not stir the mixture while it is bubbling and ensure that it does not burn.

As soon as the mixture has turned golden brown, immediately pour it on to the prepared baking tray and spread it out evenly. Leave to cool for 1 hour, or until cold and hardened. When the praline has hardened, finely crush it in a food processor or place it in a polythene bag and crush with a hammer.

To prepare the ice cream, put the chocolate and milk in a saucepan and heat gently, stirring, until the chocolate has melted and the mixture is smooth. Remove from the heat.

Put the sugar and egg yolks in a large bowl and whisk together until pale and the mixture leaves a trail when the whisk is lifted. Slowly add the milk mixture, stirring all the time with a wooden spoon. Strain the mixture into the rinsed-out saucepan or a double boiler and cook over a low heat for 10–15 minutes, stirring all the time, until the mixture thickens enough to coat the back of the spoon. Do not allow the mixture to boil or it will curdle.

Remove the custard from the heat and leave to cool for at least 1 hour, stirring from time to time to prevent a skin from forming. Meanwhile, whip the cream until it holds its shape. Keep in the refrigerator until ready to use.

If using an ice cream machine, fold the cold custard into the whipped cream, then churn the mixture in the machine following the manufacturer's instructions. Just before the ice cream freezes, add the praline. Alternatively, freeze the custard in a freezerproof container, uncovered, for 1–2 hours, or until it begins to set around the edges. Turn the custard into a bowl and stir with a fork or beat in a food processor until smooth. Fold in the whipped cream and praline. Return to the freezer and freeze for a further 2–3 hours, or until firm or required. Cover the container with a lid for storing.

With the addition of chocolate pieces and the chocolate fudge sauce, this is a popular ice cream with children. You could use a 100-g/3½-oz packet of chocolate chips instead of chopping the chocolate by hand.

Chocolate Chip Ice Cream with Hot Chocolate Fudge Sauce

INGREDIENTS
300 ml/10 fl oz full-fat milk
1 vanilla pod
115 g/4 oz milk chocolate
85 g/3 oz caster sugar
3 egg yolks
300 ml/10 fl oz whipping cream
CHOCOLATE FUDGE SAUCE
50 g/1¾ oz milk chocolate, broken
    into pieces
25 g/1 oz butter
4 tbsp full-fat milk
225 g/8 oz soft light brown sugar
2 tbsp golden syrup

SERVES 4–6

Pour the milk into a heavy-based saucepan, add the vanilla pod and bring almost to the boil. Remove from the heat and leave to infuse for 30 minutes. Meanwhile, chop the chocolate into small pieces and set aside.

Put the sugar and egg yolks in a large bowl and whisk together until pale and the mixture leaves a trail when the whisk is lifted. Remove the vanilla pod from the milk, then slowly add the milk to the sugar mixture, stirring all the time with a wooden spoon. Strain the mixture into the rinsed-out saucepan or a double boiler and cook over a low heat for 10–15 minutes, stirring all the time, until the mixture thickens enough to coat the back of the spoon. Do not boil or it will curdle.

Remove the custard from the heat and leave to cool for at least 1 hour, stirring from time to time to prevent a skin from forming. Meanwhile, whip the cream until it holds its shape. Keep in the refrigerator until ready to use.

If using an ice cream machine, fold the cold custard into the whipped cream, then churn the mixture in the machine following the manufacturer's instructions. Just before the ice cream freezes, add the chocolate pieces. Alternatively, freeze the custard in a freezerproof container, uncovered, for 1–2 hours, or until it begins to set around the edges. Turn the custard into a bowl and stir with a fork or beat in a food processor until smooth. Fold in the whipped cream and chocolate pieces. Return to the freezer and freeze for a further 2–3 hours, or until firm or required. Cover the container with a lid for storing.

Make the chocolate sauce just before you serve the ice cream. Put the chocolate, butter and milk in a heatproof bowl set over a saucepan of simmering water and heat gently, stirring occasionally, until the chocolate has melted and the sauce is smooth. Transfer the mixture to a heavy-based saucepan and stir in the sugar and syrup. Heat gently until the sugar has dissolved, then bring to the boil and boil, without stirring, for 5 minutes. Serve the hot sauce poured over the ice cream.

A traditional English ice cream that was popular at the end of the eighteenth century, the Victorians liked to decorate it with crystallized violets. There's no reason why you shouldn't do the same.

Brown Bread
Ice Cream

SERVES 4–6

Preheat the oven to 200°C/400°F/Gas Mark 6. Oil a baking tray, then spread the breadcrumbs out on the tray and sprinkle over the brown sugar. Bake in the oven for 10–15 minutes, stirring occasionally, until the breadcrumbs are golden brown and the sugar has caramelized. Leave the breadcrumbs to cool.

When the breadcrumbs are cool, using a fork, break up into crumbs again. Pour the double and single cream into a large bowl and whip together until the mixture holds its shape. Sift over the icing sugar, then fold into the cream with the vanilla essence and rum, sherry or Madeira, if using.

If using an ice cream machine, fold the breadcrumbs into the cream mixture, then churn in the machine following the manufacturer's instructions. Alternatively, freeze the cream mixture in a freezerproof container, uncovered, for 1–2 hours, or until it begins to set around the edges. Turn the mixture into a bowl and stir with a fork or beat in a food processor until smooth. Stir in the breadcrumbs. Return the ice cream to the freezer and freeze for a further 2–3 hours, or until firm or required. Cover the container with a lid for storing.

INGREDIENTS

vegetable oil, for oiling

115 g/4 oz fresh coarse-textured wholemeal breadcrumbs

55 g/2 oz soft light brown sugar

300 ml/10 fl oz double cream

150 ml/5 fl oz single cream

55 g/2 oz icing sugar

½ tsp vanilla essence

1 tbsp rum, sherry or Madeira (optional)

This is India's classic ice cream, which is traditionally served at wedding banquets. It derives its rich, characteristic caramel flavour from the milk being cooked for a long time.

Indian Kulfi

INGREDIENTS

1.4 litres/2½ pints full-fat milk

12 cardamom pods

175 g/6 oz caster sugar

115 g/4 oz shelled pistachio nuts

55 g/2 oz ground almonds, plus extra to serve

150 ml/5 fl oz double cream

SERVES 6

Pour the milk into a large heavy-based saucepan and add the cardamom pods. Bring to the boil, then reduce the heat and simmer for 45 minutes, or until reduced by half. When the milk has reduced, add the sugar and stir until dissolved. Pour the mixture into a bowl and leave to cool. When cold, chill in the refrigerator for at least 8 hours or overnight.

Meanwhile, put the pistachio nuts in a bowl and pour over enough boiling water to cover. Leave for 1–2 minutes, then drain well. With your fingers, rub off the skins, then slice the pistachio nuts into thin slivers.

When the milk mixture has chilled, strain it through a sieve to remove the cardamom pods. Stir in the ground almonds. Whip the cream until it just holds its shape, then fold into the milk mixture.

If using an ice cream machine, churn the mixture in the machine following the manufacturer's instructions. Just before the ice cream freezes, add half the slivered pistachio nuts. Alternatively, freeze the mixture in a freezerproof container, uncovered, for 1–2 hours, or until it begins to set around the edges.

Turn the mixture into a bowl and stir with a fork or beat in a food processor until smooth. Fold in the whipped cream and half of the slivered pistachio nuts. Return to the freezer and freeze for a further 2–3 hours, or until firm or required. Cover the container with a lid for storing. Serve with the remaining slivered pistachio nuts sprinkled over the top to decorate.

The short cut of using prepared fresh custard instead of making your own makes this ice cream recipe an easy option. Choose a custard that contains fresh cream or is thick and creamy.

Cinnamon Ice Cream

SERVES 4–6

Pour the cream into a heavy-based saucepan, add the cinnamon and stir together. Bring almost to the boil, then remove from the heat and leave to infuse for 30 minutes.

Put the custard and lemon juice in a large bowl. Sift in the icing sugar, then stir together. Pour in the cinnamon cream and whisk together until well mixed.

If using an ice cream machine, churn the mixture in the machine following the manufacturer's instructions. Alternatively, freeze the mixture in a freezerproof container, uncovered, for 1–2 hours, or until it begins to set around the edges. Turn the mixture into a bowl and stir with a fork or beat in a food processor until smooth. Return to the freezer and freeze for a further 2–3 hours, or until firm or required. Cover the container with a lid for storing.

INGREDIENTS
300 ml/10 fl oz whipping cream
1 tsp ground cinnamon
500-ml/18-fl oz carton fresh custard
1 tbsp lemon juice
50 g/1¾ oz icing sugar

When you have finished with the vanilla pod, don't discard it. Rinse it under cold water, leave to dry, then place it in a jar of caster sugar to make your own vanilla sugar.

Rich Vanilla Ice Cream

INGREDIENTS
300 ml/10 fl oz single cream and
   300 ml/10 fl oz double cream or
   600 ml/1 pint whipping cream
1 vanilla pod
4 large egg yolks
115 g/4 oz caster sugar

SERVES 4–6
Pour the single and double cream or whipping cream into a large heavy-based saucepan. Split open the vanilla pod and scrape out the seeds into the cream, then add the whole vanilla pod too. Bring almost to the boil, then remove from the heat and leave to infuse for 30 minutes.

Put the egg yolks and sugar in a large bowl and whisk together until pale and the mixture leaves a trail when the whisk is lifted. Remove the vanilla pod from the cream, then slowly add the cream to the egg mixture, stirring all the time with a wooden spoon. Strain the mixture into the rinsed-out saucepan or a double boiler and cook over a low heat for 10–15 minutes, stirring all the time, until the mixture thickens enough to coat the back of the spoon. Do not allow the mixture to boil or it will curdle. Remove the custard from the heat and leave to cool for at least 1 hour, stirring from time to time to prevent a skin from forming.

If using an ice cream machine, churn the cold custard in the machine following the manufacturer's instructions. Alternatively, freeze the custard in a freezerproof container, uncovered, for 1–2 hours, or until it begins to set around the edges. Turn the custard into a bowl and stir with a fork or beat in a food processor until smooth. Return to the freezer and freeze for a further 2–3 hours, or until firm or required. Cover the container with a lid for storing.

You could use instant coffee granules instead of the freshly ground coffee but the flavour will not be so distinctive.

Cappuccino Ice Cream

SERVES 4

Pour the milk and 450 ml/16 fl oz of the cream into a heavy-based saucepan, stir in the coffee and bring almost to the boil. Remove from the heat, leave to infuse for 5 minutes, then strain through a filter paper or a sieve lined with muslin.

Put the egg yolks and sugar in a large bowl and whisk together until pale and creamy. Slowly add the milk mixture, stirring all the time with a wooden spoon. Strain the mixture into the rinsed-out saucepan or a double boiler and cook over a low heat for 10–15 minutes, stirring all the time, until the mixture thickens enough to coat the back of the spoon. Do not allow the mixture to boil or it will curdle. Remove the custard from the heat and leave to cool for at least 1 hour, stirring from time to time to prevent a skin from forming.

If using an ice cream machine, churn the cold custard in the machine following the manufacturer's instructions. Alternatively, freeze the custard in a freezerproof container, uncovered, for 1–2 hours, or until it begins to set around the edges. Turn the custard into a bowl and stir with a fork or beat in a food processor until smooth. Return to the freezer and freeze for a further 2–3 hours, or until firm or required. Cover the container with a lid for storing.

To serve, whip the remaining cream until it holds its shape. Scoop the ice cream into wide-brimmed coffee cups and smooth the tops. Spoon the whipped cream over the top of each and sprinkle with cocoa powder. Decorate with chocolate-coated coffee beans.

INGREDIENTS

150 ml/5 fl oz pint full-fat milk
600 ml/1 pint whipping cream
4 tbsp finely ground fresh coffee
3 large egg yolks
115 g/4 oz caster sugar
cocoa powder, for dusting
chocolate-coated coffee beans,
    to decorate

This recipe uses evaporated milk instead of a custard base. Keep a can in the refrigerator so that the evaporated milk is chilled and ready for use. This is important for enabling the milk to be whisked.

Maple Syrup & Walnut Ice Cream

INGREDIENTS
100 g/3½ oz walnut pieces
150 ml/5 fl oz maple syrup
300 ml/10 fl oz double cream
200 ml/7 fl oz canned evaporated milk,
    well chilled

SERVES 6
Put the walnut pieces in a food processor and process until finely chopped but be careful not to process them into a purée. Set aside.

Mix the syrup and cream together until well blended. Pour the chilled evaporated milk into a large bowl and whisk until thick and doubled in volume. The mixture should leave a trail when the whisk is lifted. Add the syrup mixture to the whisked milk and fold together.

If using an ice cream machine, churn the mixture in the machine following the manufacturer's instructions. Just before the ice cream freezes, add the chopped nuts. Alternatively, freeze the mixture in a freezerproof container, uncovered, for 1–2 hours, or until it begins to set around the edges. Turn the mixture into a bowl and stir with a fork or beat in a food processor until smooth. Stir in the chopped nuts, then return to the freezer and freeze for a further 2–3 hours, or until firm or required. Cover the container with a lid for storing.

The sauce is extremely easy to make in a microwave. Simply put all the ingredients in a medium bowl or jug and cook on High for 3 minutes, stirring several times, until melted.

Ginger Ice Cream with Hot Chocolate Sauce

INGREDIENTS
300 ml/10 fl oz full-fat milk

3 egg yolks

85 g/3 oz soft light brown sugar

300 ml/10 fl oz whipping cream

55 g/1¾ oz stem ginger

1 tbsp stem ginger syrup

HOT CHOCOLATE SAUCE

175 g/6 oz plain dark chocolate, broken
   into pieces

25 g/1 oz butter

3 tbsp golden syrup

3 tbsp full-fat milk

SERVES 4–6
Pour the milk into a heavy-based saucepan and bring almost to the boil. Remove from the heat. Put the egg yolks and sugar in a large bowl and whisk together until pale and the mixture leaves a trail when the whisk is lifted. Slowly add the milk, stirring all the time with a wooden spoon. Strain the mixture into the rinsed-out saucepan or a double boiler and cook over a low heat for 10–15 minutes, stirring all the time, until the mixture thickens enough to coat the back of the spoon. Do not allow the mixture to boil or it will curdle. Remove the custard from the heat and leave to cool for at least 1 hour, stirring from time to time to prevent a skin from forming.

Meanwhile, whip the cream until it holds its shape. Keep in the refrigerator until ready to use. Finely chop the stem ginger. When the custard is cold, stir the stem ginger syrup into it but not the chopped ginger at this stage.

If using an ice cream machine, fold the cold custard into the whipped cream, then churn the mixture in the machine following the manufacturer's instructions. Just before the ice cream freezes, add the chopped stem ginger. Alternatively, freeze the custard in a freezerproof container, uncovered, for 1–2 hours, or until it begins to set around the edges. Turn the custard into a bowl and stir with a fork or beat in a food processor until smooth. Fold in the whipped cream and chopped stem ginger. Return to the freezer and freeze for a further 2–3 hours, or until firm or required. Cover the container with a lid for storing.

Make the hot chocolate sauce just before you are going to serve the ice cream. Put the ingredients in a heatproof bowl set over a saucepan of simmering water and heat gently, stirring occasionally, until the chocolate has melted and the sauce is smooth. Serve the hot sauce poured over the ice cream.

Real Italian ice cream has a soft texture because, as in this recipe, it is made with milk and contains no cream. If you are using the green food colouring, add it very slowly, drop by drop.

Italian Pistachio Gelato

INGREDIENTS
850 ml/1½ pints full-fat milk

1 vanilla pod

9 egg yolks

175 g/6 oz caster sugar

2 tbsp almond-flavoured liqueur (optional)

few drops of green food colouring (optional)

100 g/3½ oz shelled pistachio nuts

SERVES 6–8

Pour the milk into a heavy-based saucepan, add the vanilla pod and bring almost to the boil. Remove from the heat and leave to infuse for 15 minutes.

Put the egg yolks and sugar in a large bowl and whisk together until pale and the mixture leaves a trail when the whisk is lifted. Remove the vanilla pod from the milk, then slowly add the milk to the egg mixture, stirring all the time with a wooden spoon. Strain the mixture into the rinsed-out saucepan or a double boiler and cook over a low heat for 10–15 minutes, stirring all the time, until the mixture thickens enough to coat the back of the spoon. Do not allow the mixture to boil or it will curdle.

Remove the custard from the heat and leave to cool for at least 1 hour, stirring from time to time to prevent a skin from forming. When the custard is cold, stir in the liqueur, if using, and, if wished, add the food colouring to tint the mixture pale green. Finely chop the nuts.

If using an ice cream machine, churn the cold custard in the machine following the manufacturer's instructions. Just before the ice cream freezes, add the chopped nuts. Alternatively, freeze the custard in a freezerproof container, uncovered, for 1–2 hours, or until it begins to set around the edges. Turn the custard into a bowl and stir with a fork or beat in a food processor until smooth. Stir in the chopped nuts, then return to the freezer and freeze for a further 2–3 hours, or until firm or required. Cover the container with a lid for storing.

the fru

the fruit bowl

Fresh fruit desserts are always popular, and soft berries and citrus fruits all blend beautifully with fresh cream and yogurt to make luscious fruit ice creams. The only rule is that you must choose the freshest, ripest, most unblemished fruits. Make the recipes to be found here when the fruits are in season and plentiful. From Rippled Blackcurrant Ice Cream to Fresh Peach Ice Cream and Crushed Cherry Ice Cream to Dairy Strawberry Ice Cream, you can provide instant desserts throughout the summer.

Fruit ice creams in particular look stunning and impressive when served in an ice bowl inlaid with fresh fruit and leaves. An ice bowl is surprisingly easy to make: take a 1.5-litre/2¾-pint pudding bowl and, if wished, line the base and sides with slices of orange or lemon and mint, lemon balm or scented geranium leaves. Insert a 1-litre/1¾-pint pudding bowl inside and fill the space between the two bowls with water. Immediately place a plate and a heavy weight on top. Put in the freezer for at least 4 hours, until frozen or required. To use the ice bowl, run the bowls under hot water until they loosen, then quickly transfer the ice bowl to a serving plate and return to the freezer until ready to fill.

For an attractive finishing touch, serve the ice creams with more of the fresh fruits from which they were made. A few fresh strawberries, some orange segments, a scattering of raspberries or a whole cherry popped on top makes all the difference.

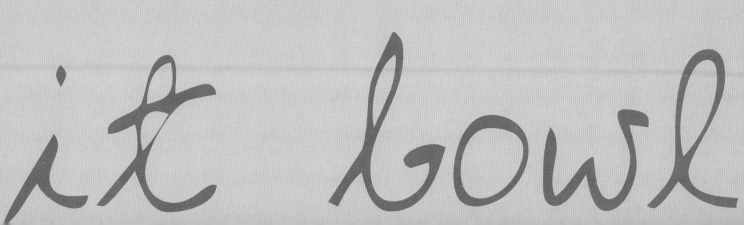

Other varieties of rippled fruit ice cream, such as raspberry and strawberry, can be made in the same way. Simply substitute the blackcurrants with your chosen fruit.

Rippled Blackcurrant Ice Cream

INGREDIENTS
425 ml/15 fl oz full-fat milk

1 vanilla pod

250 g/9 oz caster sugar

4 egg yolks

350 g/12 oz fresh blackcurrants, plus extra to decorate

6 tbsp water

425 ml/15 fl oz whipping cream

SERVES 6–8

Pour the milk into a heavy-based saucepan, add the vanilla pod and bring almost to the boil. Remove from the heat and leave to infuse for 30 minutes. Put 125 g/4½ oz of the sugar and the egg yolks in a large bowl and whisk together until pale and the mixture leaves a trail when the whisk is lifted. Remove the vanilla pod from the milk, then slowly add the milk to the sugar mixture, stirring all the time with a wooden spoon. Strain the mixture into the rinsed-out saucepan or a double boiler and cook over a low heat for 10–15 minutes, stirring all the time, until the mixture thickens enough to coat the back of the spoon. Do not allow the mixture to boil or it will curdle. Remove the custard from the heat and leave to cool for at least 1 hour, stirring from time to time to prevent a skin from forming.

Meanwhile, strip the blackcurrants from their stalks using the prongs of a fork and put them in a heavy-based saucepan with the remaining sugar and the water. Heat gently, stirring, until the sugar has dissolved, then simmer gently for 10 minutes, or until the blackcurrants are very soft.

Push the blackcurrants through a nylon sieve into a bowl to remove the seeds, then leave the purée to cool. Meanwhile, whip the cream until it holds its shape. Keep in the refrigerator until ready to use.

If using an ice cream machine, fold the cold custard into the whipped cream, then churn the mixture in the machine following the manufacturer's instructions. Just before the ice cream freezes, spread half in a freezerproof container. Pour

over half the blackcurrant purée, then repeat the layers. Freeze for 1–2 hours, or until firm or required. Alternatively, freeze the custard in a freezerproof container, uncovered, for 1–2 hours, or until it begins to set around the edges. Turn the custard into a bowl and stir with a fork or beat in a food processor until smooth. Fold in the whipped cream. Spread half back into the container, then pour over half the blackcurrant purée. Repeat the layers. Return to the freezer and freeze for 2–3 hours, or until firm or required. Cover the container with a lid for storing. Serve decorated with blackcurrants.

The Greek yogurt makes this smooth and creamy, and the lemon juice imparts a fresh tang. For an orange version, use 6 tablespoons of frozen concentrated, unsweetened orange juice instead of lemon juice.

Greek Lemon Yogurt Ice Cream

INGREDIENTS
2–3 lemons
500-ml/18-fl oz carton authentic
  Greek yogurt
150 m/5 fl oz double cream
100 g/3½ oz caster sugar
finely pared lemon rind, to decorate

SERVES 4–6

Squeeze the juice from the lemons – you need 6 tablespoons in total. Put the juice into a bowl, add the yogurt, cream and sugar and mix well together.

If using an ice cream machine, churn the mixture in the machine following the manufacturer's instructions. Alternatively, freeze the mixture in a freezerproof container, uncovered, for 1–2 hours, or until it begins to set around the edges. Turn the mixture into a bowl and stir with a fork or beat in a food processor until smooth. Return to the freezer and freeze for a further 2–3 hours, or until firm or required. Cover the container with a lid for storing. Serve with finely pared lemon rind.

When choosing shop-bought ice cream, always buy a variety that is described as 'dairy'. This contains a proportion of double cream, as opposed to others that are made with only vegetable fat.

Dairy Strawberry Ice Cream

SERVES 6

Put the sugar and water in a heavy-based saucepan and heat gently, stirring, until the sugar has dissolved. Bring to the boil, then, without stirring, boil for 5 minutes to form a syrup. Towards the end of the cooking time, keep an eye on the mixture to ensure that it does not burn. Immediately remove the syrup from the heat and leave to cool for at least 1 hour.

Meanwhile, push the strawberries through a nylon sieve into a bowl to form a purée. When the syrup is cold, add the strawberry purée to it with the lemon juice and orange juice and stir well together. Whip the cream until it holds its shape. Keep in the refrigerator until ready to use.

If using an ice cream machine, fold the strawberry mixture into the whipped cream, then churn in the machine following the manufacturer's instructions. Alternatively, freeze the mixture in a freezerproof container, uncovered, for 1–2 hours, or until it begins to set around the edges. Turn the mixture into a bowl and stir with a fork or beat in a food processor until smooth. Fold in the whipped cream. Return to the freezer and freeze for a further 2–3 hours, or until firm or required. Cover the container with a lid for storing. Serve decorated with strawberries.

INGREDIENTS
225 g/8 oz caster sugar
150 ml/5 fl oz water
900 g/2 lb fresh strawberries, plus extra to decorate
juice of ½ lemon
juice of ½ orange
300ml/10 fl oz whipping cream

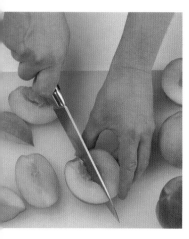

A delightful ice cream to serve in summer, this recipe uses condensed milk instead of custard, which makes it very simple and quick to prepare.

Fresh Peach Ice Cream

INGREDIENTS
4 ripe peaches
300 ml/10 fl oz canned condensed milk
juice of 1 lemon
300 ml/10 fl oz whipping cream
toasted flaked almonds, to decorate

SERVES 6

Cut the peaches into quarters with a sharp knife, remove the stones, then peel off the skins. Roughly chop the peach flesh.

Put the chopped peaches, condensed milk and lemon juice in a food processor or blender and process to form a purée. Push the mixture through a fine nylon sieve into a bowl to remove the brown flecks of flesh. Whip the cream until it holds its shape. Keep in the refrigerator until ready to use.

If using an ice cream machine, fold the whipped cream into the peach mixture, then churn in the machine following the manufacturer's instructions. Alternatively, freeze the mixture in a freezerproof container, uncovered, for 1–2 hours, or until it begins to set around the edges. Turn the mixture into a bowl and stir with a fork or beat in a food processor until smooth. Fold in the whipped cream. Return to the freezer and freeze for a further 2–3 hours, or until firm or required. Cover the container with a lid for storing. Serve decorated with toasted flaked almonds.

To serve this ice cream in the empty orange halves, cut around the inside of the oranges with a serrated knife and scoop out the flesh. Keep the orange shells in the freezer until you are ready.

Orange Ice Cream

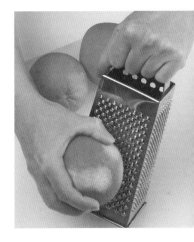

SERVES 6–8

Pour the milk into a saucepan and bring almost to the boil. Remove from the heat. Put the sugar and egg yolks in a large bowl and whisk together until pale and the mixture leaves a trail when the whisk is lifted. Slowly add the milk, stirring all the time with a wooden spoon. Strain the mixture into the rinsed-out saucepan or a double boiler and cook over a low heat for 10–15 minutes, stirring all the time, until the mixture thickens enough to coat the back of the spoon. Do not allow the mixture to boil or it will curdle. Remove the custard from the heat and leave to cool for at least 1 hour, stirring from time to time to prevent a skin from forming.

Meanwhile, finely grate the rind from 1 of the oranges and squeeze the juice from all 3 oranges – you should have about 350 ml/12 fl oz of juice in total. If wished, reserve the orange skins for serving (see above). Whip the cream until it just holds its shape. Keep in the refrigerator until ready to use. When the custard is cold, add the orange rind and juice and mix well together.

If using an ice cream machine, fold the cold custard into the whipped cream, then churn the mixture in the machine following the manufacturer's instructions. Alternatively, freeze the custard in a freezerproof container, uncovered, for 1–2 hours, or until it begins to set around the edges. Turn the custard into a bowl and stir with a fork or beat in a food processor until smooth. Fold in the whipped cream. Return to the freezer and freeze for a further 2–3 hours, or until firm or required. Cover the container with a lid for storing. Serve with the orange segments.

INGREDIENTS

300 ml/10 fl oz full-fat milk

85 g/3 oz caster sugar

3 egg yolks

300 ml/10 fl oz double cream

3 large oranges, plus 3 extra oranges, segmented, to serve

It is the Italian mascarpone cheese that gives this ice cream its creaminess, but any other rich, fresh cheese can be used. Bottled lime juice, instead of fresh, makes it simple to prepare.

Lime & Mascarpone Ice Cream

INGREDIENTS
125 ml/4 fl oz bottled lime juice
   or cordial
500 g/1 lb 2 oz mascarpone cheese
175 g/6 oz icing sugar
150 ml/5 fl oz whipping cream

SERVES 4–6
Put the lime juice in a bowl, add the mascarpone and beat together. Sift the icing sugar into the mixture and beat again until well blended. Whip the cream until it holds its shape. Keep in the refrigerator until ready to use.

If using an ice cream machine, fold the whipped cream into the mascarpone mixture, then churn in the machine following the manufacturer's instructions. Alternatively, freeze the mixture in a freezerproof container, uncovered, for 1–2 hours, or until it begins to set around the edges. Turn the mixture into a bowl and stir with a fork or beat in a food processor until smooth. Fold in the whipped cream. Return to the freezer and freeze for a further 2–3 hours, or until firm or required. Cover the container with a lid for storing.

This is a very rich ice cream. Omit the rum if serving it to children. You can make Avocado Ice Cream following the same recipe. Simply replace the bananas with 2 large avocados.

Banana Ice Cream

SERVES 8

Peel and slice the bananas, then put the flesh in a food processor or blender. Add the lemon juice and process to form a very smooth purée. Turn the mixture into a large bowl. Alternatively, sprinkle the lemon juice over the banana slices, then push the flesh through a nylon sieve to form a purée. Add the rum, if using, and mix well together.

Sift the icing sugar into the mixture and beat until well mixed. Whip the cream until it holds its shape. Keep in the refrigerator until ready to use.

If using an ice cream machine, fold the whipped cream into the banana mixture, then churn the mixture in the machine following the manufacturer's instructions. Alternatively, freeze the mixture in a freezerproof container, uncovered, for 1–2 hours, or until it begins to set around the edges. Turn the mixture into a bowl and stir with a fork or beat in a food processor until smooth. Fold in the whipped cream. Return to the freezer and freeze for a further 2–3 hours, or until firm or required. Cover the container with a lid for storing.

INGREDIENTS
3 bananas
2 tbsp lemon juice
1 tbsp white rum (optional)
115 g/4 oz icing sugar
600 ml/1 pint whipping cream

If you have a fresh coconut, its grated flesh can be used instead of the desiccated coconut. Malibu is a coconut-flavoured liqueur, which blends well with the ice cream, but you could use white rum.

Coconut Ice Cream with Tropical Fruits

INGREDIENTS
600 ml/1 pint coconut milk
175 g/6 oz caster sugar
6 egg yolks
175 g/6 oz desiccated coconut
150 ml/5 fl oz double cream
1 tbsp Malibu (optional)
TROPICAL FRUITS
2 pawpaws, peeled and seeded
2 star fruit
2 kiwi fruit, peeled
1 tbsp caster sugar
4 tbsp Malibu (optional)

SERVES 6

Pour the coconut milk into a saucepan and heat gently. Remove from the heat. Put the sugar and egg yolks in a large bowl and whisk together until pale and the mixture leaves a trail when the whisk is lifted. Slowly add the coconut milk, stirring all the time with a wooden spoon. Strain the mixture into the rinsed-out saucepan or a double boiler and cook over a low heat for 10–15 minutes, stirring all the time, until the mixture thickens enough to coat the back of the spoon. You may find that the mixture starts to separate, and if it does, simply whisk it vigorously until it is smooth again. Do not allow the mixture to boil or it will curdle.

Remove the custard from the heat, stir in the desiccated coconut, then leave to cool for at least 1 hour, stirring from time to time to prevent a skin from forming.

Meanwhile, whip the cream until it just holds its shape. Keep in the refrigerator until ready to use. When the custard is cold, add the Malibu, if using, and mix well together.

If using an ice cream machine, fold the cold custard into the whipped cream, then churn the mixture in the machine following the manufacturer's instructions. Alternatively, freeze the custard in a freezerproof container, uncovered, for 1–2 hours, or until it begins to set around the edges. Turn the custard into a bowl and stir with a fork or beat in a food processor until smooth. Fold in the whipped cream. Return to the freezer and freeze for a further 2–3 hours, or until firm or required. Cover the container with a lid for storing.

To prepare the tropical fruits, thinly slice and put in a large shallow dish. Sprinkle the sugar and Malibu, if using, over the fruit, then cover and chill in the refrigerator for 2–3 hours before serving with the ice cream.

To make a raspberry or strawberry version, replace the cherries with the appropriate fresh fruit. For a peach or apricot version, use 425 g/15 oz canned fruit in syrup and 150 ml/5 fl oz of the syrup.

Crushed Cherry Ice Cream

SERVES 6

Put the sugar and water in a heavy-based saucepan and heat gently, stirring, until the sugar has dissolved, then bring to the boil and boil for 3 minutes. Reduce the heat, add the cherries and simmer gently for about 10 minutes, or until soft. Leave the mixture to cool for at least 1 hour.

When the cherries are cold, put them in a food processor or blender with the syrup. Add the orange juice and process the cherries until just roughly chopped. Do not blend too much as the cherries should just be crushed, not puréed. Pour the double and single cream into a large bowl and whip together until the mixture holds its shape. Fold in the crushed cherries.

If using an ice cream machine, churn the mixture in the machine following the manufacturer's instructions. Alternatively, freeze the mixture in a freezerproof container, uncovered, for 1–2 hours, or until it begins to set around the edges. Turn the mixture into a bowl and stir with a fork or beat in a food processor until smooth. Return to the freezer and freeze for a further 2–3 hours, or until firm or required. Cover the container with a lid for storing. Serve decorated with whole cherries.

INGREDIENTS
115 g/4 oz sugar
150 ml/5 fl oz water
225 g/8 oz fresh cherries, stoned, plus
    extra whole cherries to decorate
2 tbsp freshly squeezed orange juice
300 ml/10 fl oz double cream
150 ml/5 fl oz single cream

Cream Crowdie is often considered the national pudding of Scotland. It consists of oatmeal, double cream and Drambuie with optional raspberries. Here the pudding has been turned into an ice cream.

Cream Crowdie Ice Cream

INGREDIENTS
75 g/2¾ oz coarse oatmeal
600 ml/1 pint whipping cream
115 g/4 oz caster sugar
2 tbsp Drambuie
2 tbsp honey (preferably heather)
150 g/5½ oz fresh raspberries,
    plus extra to decorate

SERVES 6
Preheat the oven to 180°C/350°F/Gas Mark 4. Spread the oatmeal out on a baking tray and bake in the oven for about 10 minutes, tossing the oatmeal several times during the cooking time so that it browns evenly. Remove from the oven and leave to cool for 30 minutes.

Pour the cream into a large bowl, add the sugar and whip until the cream holds its shape. Add the Drambuie and honey and fold in until well blended.

If using an ice cream machine, churn the mixture in the machine following the manufacturer's instructions. Just before the ice cream freezes, add the toasted oatmeal and raspberries. Alternatively, freeze the mixture in a freezerproof container, uncovered, for 1–2 hours, or until it begins to set around the edges. Turn the mixture into a bowl and stir with a fork or beat in a food processor until smooth. Fold in the toasted oatmeal and the raspberries, then return to the freezer and freeze for a further 2–3 hours, or until firm or required. Cover the container with a lid for storing. Serve scattered with raspberries.

all iced up

Clean-tasting sorbets, or water ices, make a refreshing dessert to finish a rich meal, but they can also be served between courses to cleanse the palate. Savoury sorbets, such as the Fresh Mint Sorbet, can be served as a starter. Sorbets are made from a sugar syrup, flavoured with fruit juice, fruit purée, wine, liqueur, tea or herbs and sometimes contain egg whites to make them lighter. A wide variety of sorbets can be found in this chapter, for example Coffee Granita, an Italian water ice that is served broken into small ice crystals, and Gooseberry and Elderflower Sherbet, which is slightly creamy but not as creamy as an ice cream.

Like ice creams, sorbets made in the freezer need to be beaten during the freezing process to produce a smooth texture. If you own an ice cream machine, then this is done for you. If you don't and you would rather not have to return to the freezer to beat the mixture, then try the recipe for Raspberry Parfait where the beating is done at the preparation stage.

Made in a machine, sorbets can be served freshly churned, but if frozen in the freezer, they need to be left to soften for about 10 minutes at room temperature prior to serving. Sorbets look their most elegant when served in individual glasses. If convenient, they can be scooped out well ahead of time and stored in the freezer on trays lined with non-stick baking paper. The scoops can then be piled into chilled glasses and served.

A particularly refreshing sorbet, it is ideal served as a starter or a palate-cleanser between courses. If wished, extra chopped fresh mint can be stirred in just before it freezes firmly.

Fresh Mint Sorbet

SERVES 4–6

Put the sugar and water in a heavy-based saucepan and heat gently, stirring, until the sugar has dissolved. Bring to the boil, then cook, without stirring, over a medium heat for 2 minutes. Remove from the heat and leave to cool slightly.

Meanwhile, strip the mint leaves from their stems and put the leaves in a food processor. Pour the syrup over the mint leaves, then process until they are very finely chopped. Leave to cool, then chill the mint syrup in the refrigerator for 2 hours, or until cold.

Squeeze the juice from the lemons and measure out 125 ml/4 fl oz. Add the juice to the mint syrup, then strain the mixture through a nylon sieve.

If using an ice cream machine, churn the mixture in the machine following the manufacturer's instructions. Alternatively, freeze the mixture in a freezerproof container, uncovered, for 3–4 hours, or until mushy. Turn the mixture into a bowl and stir with a fork or beat in a food processor to break down the ice crystals. Return the sorbet to the freezer and freeze for a further 3–4 hours, or until firm or required. Cover the container with a lid for storing. Serve decorated with mint sprigs.

INGREDIENTS
225 g/8 oz sugar
300 ml/10 fl oz water
60 g/2¼ oz fresh mint, plus extra
    sprigs to decorate
3–4 lemons

Choose mangoes that are juicy and ripe to make this sorbet. To test for ripeness, smell them. A ripe mango gives off a noticeable fragrance.

Mango Sorbet

INGREDIENTS
2 large ripe mangoes
juice of 1 lemon
pinch of salt
115 g/4 oz sugar
3 tbsp water

SERVES 4–6

Using a sharp knife, thinly peel the mangoes, holding them over a bowl to catch the juices. Cut the flesh away from the central stone and put in a food processor or blender. Add the mango juice, lemon juice and salt and process to form a smooth purée. Push the mango purée through a nylon sieve into the bowl.

Put the sugar and water in a heavy-based saucepan and heat gently, stirring, until the sugar has dissolved. Bring to the boil, without stirring, then remove from the heat and leave to cool slightly.

Pour the syrup into the mango purée and mix well together. Leave to cool, then chill the mango syrup in the refrigerator for 2 hours, or until cold.

If using an ice cream machine, churn the mixture in the machine following the manufacturer's instructions. Alternatively, freeze the mixture in a freezerproof container, uncovered, for 3–4 hours, or until mushy. Turn the mixture into a bowl and stir with a fork or beat in a food processor to break down the ice crystals. Return to the freezer and freeze for a further 3–4 hours, or until firm or required. Cover the container with a lid for storing.

Granita is an Italian sorbet or water ice, which is broken into small ice crystals and served in tall glasses. It is cooling on a hot day and is a suitable dessert after a substantial dinner.

Coffee Granita

SERVES 6

Put the sugar and water in a heavy-based saucepan and heat gently, stirring, until the sugar has dissolved. Bring to the boil, then remove from the heat and stir in the coffee. Leave to infuse for 1 hour and become cold.

Strain the coffee through a filter paper or a sieve lined with muslin. Pour the coffee into 2 shallow freezerproof containers and freeze, uncovered, for 30 minutes.

Turn both mixtures into a bowl and stir with a fork, or beat in a food processor, to break down the ice crystals. Return to the freezer and freeze, repeating the breaking down of the ice crystals about every 30 minutes until the granita is granular. This process will take 3–4 hours in total. Cover the container with a lid for storing.

Serve the granita in glasses, straight from the freezer, broken into tiny ice crystals. Top each glass with a little whipped cream.

INGREDIENTS
25 g/1 oz sugar
600 ml/1 pint water
50 g/1¾ oz fresh Italian coffee, finely ground
125 ml/4 fl oz whipping cream, whipped, to serve

It is possible to use a variety of soft fruits in this recipe, although you won't necessarily end up with a red berry sorbet! Choose from strawberries, blackberries and blackcurrants.

Red Berry Sorbet

INGREDIENTS
225 g/8 oz redcurrants, plus extra
   to decorate
225 g/8 oz raspberries, plus extra
   to decorate
175 ml/6 fl oz water
115 g/4 oz sugar
150 ml/5 fl oz cranberry juice
2 egg whites

CAUTION
Recipes using raw eggs should be avoided by infants, the elderly, pregnant women, convalescents and anyone suffering from an illness.

SERVES 6

Strip the redcurrants from their stalks using the prongs of a fork and put them in a large heavy-based saucepan together with the raspberries. Add 30 ml/ 1 fl oz of the water and cook over a medium heat for 10 minutes, or until soft. Push the fruit through a nylon sieve into a bowl to form a purée.

Put the sugar and the remaining water into the rinsed-out saucepan and heat gently, stirring, until the sugar has dissolved. Bring to the boil, then boil, without stirring, for 10 minutes to form a syrup. Do not allow it to brown. Remove from the heat and leave to cool for at least 1 hour. When cold, stir the fruit purée and cranberry juice into the syrup.

If using an ice cream machine, churn the mixture in the machine following the manufacturer's instructions. When the mixture begins to freeze, whisk the egg whites until they just hold their shape but are not dry, then add to the mixture and continue churning. Alternatively, freeze the mixture in a freezerproof container, uncovered, for 3–4 hours, or until mushy. Turn the mixture into a bowl and stir with a fork or beat in a food processor to break down the ice crystals. Lightly whisk the egg whites until stiff but not dry, then fold them into the mixture. Return to the freezer and freeze for a further 3–4 hours, or until firm or required. Cover the container with a lid for storing. Serve scattered with extra fruits.

The recipe suggests pushing the kiwi fruit purée through a sieve to remove the seeds, but, if you prefer, you can omit this so that the sorbet is flecked with the dark seeds.

Kiwi Fruit Sorbet

SERVES 6

Put the sugar and water in a heavy-based saucepan and heat gently, stirring, until the sugar has dissolved. Bring to the boil, then simmer, without stirring, for 2 minutes. Remove from the heat and leave to cool for at least 1 hour.

Using a sharp knife, thinly peel the kiwi fruit. Put the flesh in a food processor or blender, add the syrup and process to form a smooth purée. Push the purée through a nylon sieve into a bowl to remove the seeds, if preferred.

If using an ice cream machine, churn the mixture in the machine following the manufacturer's instructions. When the mixture begins to freeze, whisk the egg whites until they just hold their shape but are not dry, then add to the mixture and continue churning. Alternatively, freeze the mixture in a freezerproof container, uncovered, for 3 hours, or until mushy. Turn the mixture into a bowl and stir with a fork or beat in a food processor to break down the ice crystals. Lightly whisk the egg whites until stiff but not dry, then fold them into the mixture. Return the sorbet to the freezer and freeze for a further 3–4 hours, or until firm or required. Cover the container with a lid for storing. Serve decorated with the extra kiwi fruit, peeled and sliced.

INGREDIENTS
55 g/2 oz sugar
150 ml/5 fl oz water
8 kiwi fruit, plus 2 extra to decorate
2 egg whites

CAUTION
Recipes using raw eggs should be avoided by infants, the elderly, pregnant women, convalescents and anyone suffering from an illness.

The lemon rind and juice added to the basic sugar syrup complement the delicate flavour of the passion fruit extremely well. The addition of gelatine helps to produce a smooth texture.

Passion Fruit Sorbet

INGREDIENTS
350 ml/12 fl oz water
1 tsp powdered gelatine
250 g/9 oz sugar
grated rind and juice of 2 lemons
8 passion fruit, plus 2 extra, to serve

SERVES 6

Put 2 tablespoons of the water in a small bowl and sprinkle in the gelatine. Leave to soak for 5 minutes.

Meanwhile, put the remaining water, the sugar and lemon rind in a heavy-based saucepan and heat gently, stirring, until the sugar has dissolved. Bring to the boil, then simmer, without stirring, for 2 minutes. Remove from the heat.

Add the soaked gelatine to the syrup and stir until dissolved. Stir in the lemon juice. Cut the passion fruit in half and, holding them over the syrup, scoop out the seeds with a teaspoon into the syrup. Leave the syrup to cool, then chill in the refrigerator for 2 hours, or until cold. When cold, strain the syrup through a nylon sieve into a bowl.

If using an ice cream machine, churn the mixture in the machine following the manufacturer's instructions. Alternatively, freeze the mixture in a freezerproof container, uncovered, for 3–4 hours, or until mushy. Turn the mixture into a bowl and stir with a fork or beat in a food processor to break down the ice crystals. Return to the freezer and freeze for a further 3–4 hours, or until firm or required. Cover the container with a lid for storing. Serve decorated with the scooped out seeds of the extra passion fruit spooned over the top.

If you would prefer the sorbet to contain lemon rind, finely grate the rind and add it to the sugar syrup — there is no need to strain it.

Lemon Water Ice

SERVES 6

Put the sugar and water in a heavy-based saucepan and heat gently, stirring, until the sugar has dissolved. Bring to the boil, then boil, without stirring, for 10 minutes to form a syrup. Do not allow it to brown.

Meanwhile, using a potato peeler, thinly pare the rind from 4 of the lemons. Remove the syrup from the heat and add the pared lemon rind. Leave to cool for at least 1 hour.

Squeeze the juice from the lemons and strain into a measuring jug — you need 425 ml/15 fl oz in total. When the syrup is cold, strain it into a bowl, add the lemon juice and stir together until well mixed.

If using an ice cream machine, churn the mixture in the machine following the manufacturer's instructions. Alternatively, freeze the mixture in a freezerproof container, uncovered, for 3–4 hours, or until mushy. Turn the mixture into a bowl and stir with a fork or beat in a food processor to break down the ice crystals. Return to the freezer and freeze for a further 3–4 hours, or until firm or required. Cover the container with a lid for storing. Serve decorated with lemon slices.

INGREDIENTS
175 g/6 oz sugar
425 ml/15 fl oz water
6–9 large lemons
lemon slices, to decorate

Gooseberries and elderflowers are perfect partners. Elderflower cordial has been used in this recipe as it is more readily available than freshly picked elderflower heads.

Gooseberry & Elderflower Sherbet

INGREDIENTS

115 g/4 oz sugar
600 ml/1 pint water
500 g/1 lb 2 oz fresh gooseberries
125 ml/4 fl oz elderflower cordial
1 tbsp lemon juice
few drops of green food colouring
(optional)
125 ml/4 fl oz double cream

SERVES 6

Put the sugar and water in a large heavy-based saucepan and heat gently, stirring, until the sugar has dissolved. Bring to the boil, then add the gooseberries, without topping and tailing them, and simmer, stirring occasionally, for 10 minutes, or until very tender. Leave to cool for 5 minutes.

Put the gooseberries in a food processor or blender and process to form a smooth purée. Push the purée through a nylon sieve into a bowl to remove the seeds. Leave to cool for at least 1 hour.

Add the elderflower cordial and lemon juice to the cold gooseberry purée and stir together until well mixed. If wished, add the food colouring to tint the mixture pale green. Stir the cream into the mixture.

If using an ice cream machine, churn the mixture in the machine following the manufacturer's instructions. Alternatively, freeze the mixture in a freezerproof container, uncovered, for 3–4 hours, or until mushy. Turn the mixture into a bowl and stir with a fork or beat in a food processor to break down the ice crystals. Return to the freezer and freeze for a further 3–4 hours, or until firm or required. Cover the container with a lid for storing.

A parfait is a rich, creamy ice. It is made from a sugar syrup, which is poured over whisked egg whites and whisked until it is thick, creamy and voluminous. It is often flavoured with a liqueur.

Raspberry Parfait

SERVES 6

Put the raspberries in a food processor or blender and process to form a smooth purée. Push through a nylon sieve into a bowl to remove the seeds. Sift the icing sugar into the raspberry purée, then stir together until well mixed. Stir in the kirsch or cherry brandy, if using.

Put the granulated sugar and water in a small heavy-based saucepan and heat gently, stirring, until the sugar has dissolved. Bring to the boil, then boil, without stirring, for 5 minutes, or until a syrup has formed. Do not allow it to brown. Meanwhile, whisk the egg whites until stiff and dry.

Drizzle the hot syrup in a thin stream on to the whisked egg whites, whisking all the time until the mixture is thick, creamy and fluffy. Continue whisking until the mixture is cold.

Whip the cream until stiff. Fold the raspberry purée into the egg white mixture, then fold in the whipped cream.

Freeze the raspberry mixture in a freezerproof container, uncovered, for 3–4 hours, or until firm or required. Cover the container with a lid for storing. Serve scattered with raspberries.

INGREDIENTS
450 g/1 lb fresh raspberries, plus extra
    to decorate
85 g/3 oz icing sugar
1 tbsp kirsch or cherry brandy (optional)
75 g/2¾ oz granulated sugar
125 ml/4 fl oz water
2 egg whites
300 ml/10 fl oz whipping cream

CAUTION
Recipes using raw eggs should be avoided by infants, the elderly, pregnant women, convalescents and anyone suffering from an illness.

This is a particularly refreshing sorbet to serve on a hot summer's day or as a dessert to follow a substantial meal. Other suitable teas are Earl Grey and peppermint.

Green Tea Sorbet

INGREDIENTS
850 ml/1½ pints water
175 g/6 oz sugar
4 tbsp Japanese green tea leaves
2 tbsp lemon juice
2 egg whites

CAUTION
Recipes using raw eggs should be avoided by infants, the elderly, pregnant women, convalescents and anyone suffering from an illness.

SERVES 6

Put 600 ml/1 pint of the water in a heavy-based saucepan, add the sugar and heat gently, stirring, until the sugar has dissolved. Bring to the boil, then simmer, without stirring, for 10 minutes to form a syrup. Do not allow it to brown. Remove from the heat and leave to cool for at least 1 hour.

Meanwhile, bring the remaining water to the boil. Pour over the tea leaves and allow to infuse for 10 minutes. Strain the tea liquid. When the syrup is cold, add the strained tea and lemon juice and stir together until well mixed.

If using an ice cream machine, churn the mixture in the machine following the manufacturer's instructions. When the mixture begins to freeze, whisk the egg whites until they just hold their shape but are not dry, then fold into the mixture and continue churning. Alternatively, freeze the mixture in a freezerproof container, uncovered, for 3–4 hours, or until mushy. Turn the mixture into a bowl and stir with a fork or beat in a food processor to break down the ice crystals. Lightly whisk the egg whites until they just hold their shape but are not dry, then fold them into the mixture. Return to the freezer and freeze for a further 3–4 hours, until firm or required. Cover the container with a lid for storing.

frozen

frozen assets

The recipes in this chapter are, as the title suggests, useful, valuable assets. The joy is that they can be made in advance and stored in the freezer. There they can be kept and brought out just before serving for a special occasion. Christmas Pudding Ice Cream falls into this category, as does Sicilian Bombe. Then there is Zabaglione Semifreddo, an impressive ice cream version of the classic Italian dessert.

These are sophisticated iced desserts. Layered, studded with fruit and nuts, packed with contrasting flavours, colours and textures, they are perfect for entertaining. You will find elegant bombes and terrines, many of which appear elaborate but are no more complicated or time-consuming to make than the other ice cream recipes in this book. Most are based on a rich egg custard, which, although it needs watching, is not difficult to make. No specific moulds are needed – ordinary pudding bowls and rectangular plastic boxes will suffice.

Don't start to panic when you come to the unmoulding stage! This can either be done as soon as you take the ice cream out of the freezer by quickly dipping the mould into hot water, or you can leave the ice cream at room temperature, then slide it out of its mould. If ice creams look a bit fuzzy around the edges, pop them back into the freezer for 5 minutes to firm up again. Turned out on to serving dishes, these are the crowning glory of ice creams. Take advantage of them.

assets

This ice cream, rich in fruit and nuts, is perfect to serve as an alternative to the traditional Christmas pudding.

Christmas Pudding Ice Cream

INGREDIENTS
50 g/1¾ oz glacé cherries
50 g/1¾ oz no-soak dried apricots
175 g/6 oz mixed dried fruit
5 tbsp sherry
450 ml/15 fl oz full-fat milk
3 eggs
125 g/4½ oz caster sugar
300 ml/10 fl oz double cream
150 ml/5 fl oz single cream
25 g/1 oz chopped blanched almonds
1 holly sprig, to decorate

SERVES 8

Halve the cherries and cut the apricots into small pieces about the same size. Put in a bowl, add the mixed dried fruit and sherry and stir together. Leave to soak for 2–3 hours, stirring occasionally, until the sherry is absorbed.

Meanwhile, pour the milk into a heavy-based saucepan and bring almost to the boil. Remove from the heat. Put the eggs and sugar in a large bowl and whisk together until pale and the mixture leaves a trail when the whisk is lifted. Slowly add the milk, stirring all the time with a wooden spoon. Strain the mixture into the rinsed-out saucepan or a double boiler and cook over a low heat for 10–15 minutes, stirring all the time, until the mixture thickens enough to coat the back of the spoon. Do not allow the mixture to boil or it will curdle. Remove the custard from the heat and leave to cool for at least 1 hour, stirring from time to time to prevent a skin from forming.

Meanwhile, whip the double cream and single cream together until the mixture holds its shape. Keep in the refrigerator until ready to use.

If using an ice cream machine, fold the cold custard into the whipped cream, then churn it in the machine following the manufacturer's instruction. Just before the ice cream freezes, turn it into a large bowl and stir in the soaked fruits and nuts. Alternatively, freeze the custard in a freezerproof container, uncovered, for 1–2 hours, or until it begins to set around the edges. Turn the custard into a bowl and stir with a fork or beat in a food processor until smooth. Fold in the whipped cream, soaked fruits and nuts. Pack the ice

cream into a 1.7-litre/3-pint pudding bowl, cover and freeze for a further 3–4 hours, or until firm or required.

Take the ice cream out of the freezer about 30 minutes before you are ready to serve it. Uncover, place a serving plate over the bowl, invert it and leave at room temperature. If it is not possible to remove the bowl by the time you wish to serve it, stand it in hot water for a few seconds to loosen it, then lift it off. Serve decorated with a sprig of holly.

This is an Italian ice cream, but 'semifreddo' means that it is softer than the traditional gelato. It is made with egg whites, which are whisked until they are stiff. Hot sugar syrup is then added.

Cassata Semifreddo

SERVES 6–8

Line a 900-g/2-lb loaf tin or 1.4-litre/2½-pint oblong freezerproof plastic container with greaseproof paper, allowing it to hang over the edges of the container so that the ice cream can be easily removed. Put the sugar and water in a small heavy-based saucepan and heat gently, stirring, until the sugar has dissolved. Bring to the boil, then boil, without stirring, for 5 minutes, or until a syrup has formed. Do not allow it to brown.

Meanwhile, whisk the egg whites until stiff and dry. Drizzle the hot syrup in a thin stream on to the whisked egg whites, whisking all the time until the mixture is thick, creamy and fluffy. Continue whisking until the mixture is cold.

Add the nuts, dried fruit and cherries to the meringue mixture and fold in until well blended. Whip the cream until it holds its shape, then fold in until well blended. Pour the mixture into the prepared tin or plastic container, cover and freeze for 5 hours, or until firm or required.

To serve the ice cream, uncover, stand the tin or plastic container in hot water for a few seconds to loosen it, then invert it on to a serving dish. Remove the greaseproof paper and, using a hot knife, cut into slices.

INGREDIENTS
115 g/4 oz granulated sugar
150 ml/5 fl oz water
2 egg whites
50 g/1¾ oz chopped blanched almonds
50 g/1¾ oz mixed dried fruit
50 g/1¾ oz glacé cherries, chopped
300 ml/10 fl oz whipping cream

CAUTION
Recipes using raw eggs should be avoided by infants, the elderly, pregnant women, convalescents and anyone suffering from an illness.

Zabaglione, the well-known Italian egg custard and Marsala dessert, is usually served immediately it is cooked but, as this recipe proves, it is also delicious served as an ice cream!

Zabaglione Semifreddo

INGREDIENTS
4 egg yolks
100 g/3½ oz caster sugar
100 ml/3½ fl oz dry Marsala
200 ml/7 fl oz whipping cream
shortbread biscuits, to serve

SERVES 4–6
Put the egg yolks and sugar in a large heatproof bowl and whisk together until pale and the mixture leaves a trail when the whisk is lifted. Whisk in the Marsala, a tablespoon at a time, until well blended.

Place the bowl over a saucepan of simmering water and heat gently, whisking all the time, until the mixture has doubled in quantity. Remove the bowl from the heat, stand the bowl in cold water and whisk until the mixture is cool.

Whip the cream until it holds its shape. Add the whipped cream to the egg mixture, then fold in until well blended.

Freeze the mixture in a freezerproof container, uncovered, for 2–3 hours, or until firm or required. Cover the container with a lid for storing.

Serve in small, tall glasses, accompanied by biscuits.

This popular Italian ice cream was created by a Mr Tortoni, who opened the first Neapolitan café in Paris in the nineteenth century, and it was here that it became famous.

Biscuit Tortoni

SERVES 6

Line a 450-g/1-lb loaf tin or 850-ml/1½-pint oblong freezerproof plastic container with greaseproof paper, allowing it to hang over the edges of the container so that the ice cream can be easily removed. Put the biscuits in a food processor and process to form fine crumbs. Alternatively, put the biscuits in a strong polythene bag and crush with a rolling pin.

Pour the double cream and single cream into a large bowl and whip together until the mixture holds its shape. Sift the icing sugar into the whipped cream, then fold in with the Marsala. Fold in the biscuits, reserving a third.

Pour the mixture into the prepared tin or plastic container, smooth the surface and freeze, uncovered, for 5 hours, or until firm or required. Cover the container with a lid for storing.

Take the ice cream out of the freezer about 30 minutes before you are ready to serve it. Uncover, turn out on to a serving dish and remove the greaseproof paper. Leave at room temperature to soften. Using a palette knife, press the reserved crushed biscuits lightly on to the top and sides of the ice cream until it is evenly coated. Serve cut into thick slices.

INGREDIENTS
125 g/4 oz amaretti biscuits
300 ml/10 fl oz double cream
150 ml/5 fl oz single cream
115 g/4 oz icing sugar
4 tbsp Marsala

Deliciously fresh-tasting, the tangy lemon and orange flavours of this ice cream combine brilliantly with the sweet caramel sauce.

Iced Citrus Terrine with Caramel Sauce

INGREDIENTS
4 egg yolks
25 g/1 oz caster sugar
300 ml/10 fl oz whipping cream
finely grated rind and juice of 1 orange
finely grated rind of 1 lemon
3 oranges, segmented, to serve
CARAMEL SAUCE
125 g/4½ oz sugar
125 ml/4 fl oz water
1 tbsp lemon juice
150 ml/5 fl oz single cream

CAUTION
Recipes using raw eggs should be avoided by infants, the elderly, pregnant women, convalescents and anyone suffering from an illness.

SERVES 6

Line a 700-g/1 lb 9-oz loaf tin or 1.2-litre/2-pint or oblong freezerproof plastic container with greaseproof paper, allowing it to hang over the edges of the container so that the ice cream can be easily removed. To make the citrus terrine, put the egg yolks and sugar in a large bowl and whisk together until pale and the mixture leaves a trail when the whisk is lifted.

Whip the cream until it holds its shape. Fold into the egg mixture, then fold in the grated orange and lemon rind and the orange juice. Do not worry if the mixture appears too runny at this stage.

Pour the mixture into the prepared tin or plastic container, cover and freeze for 4 hours, or until firm or required.

To make the caramel sauce, put the sugar, water and lemon juice in a heavy-based saucepan and heat gently, stirring, until the sugar has dissolved. Bring to the boil, then cook, without stirring, for 5 minutes, or until the mixture turns to a pale caramel colour. Remove from the heat and stir in the cream. Leave the sauce to cool, then chill in the refrigerator for at least 3 hours.

To serve the ice cream, uncover, stand the tin or plastic container in hot water for a few seconds to loosen it, then invert it on to a serving dish. Remove the greaseproof paper and, using a hot knife, cut the terrine into slices. Serve with the orange segments and accompany with the caramel sauce.

A dessert to make in the summer when raspberries are plentiful and tuck away in the freezer, to be eaten any time of year!

Raspberry Macaroon Bombe

SERVES 6

Put the biscuits in a food processor and process to form coarse crumbs. Alternatively, put the biscuits in a strong polythene bag and crush with a rolling pin. Put the crumbs in a bowl, add the kirsch and leave to soak for 30 minutes.

Meanwhile, put the raspberries in a food processor or blender and process to form a purée. Add the caster sugar and mix well together. Pour the raspberry mixture into a bowl.

Pour the double cream and single cream into a large bowl and whip together until the mixture holds its shape. Add a third of the whipped cream to the biscuit mixture and fold in until well blended. Add another third of the cream to the raspberry mixture and fold in. Sift the cocoa powder and icing sugar over the remaining third of the cream, then fold into the cream until thoroughly incorporated.

Put the macaroon mixture in the bottom of a 1.4-litre/2½-pint pudding bowl. Add the chocolate cream and spread over to form a layer, then add the raspberry mixture. Cover the bowl and freeze for 5 hours, or until firm or required.

Take the ice cream out of the freezer about 30 minutes before you are ready to serve it. Uncover, place a serving plate over the bowl, invert it and leave at room temperature. If it is not possible to remove the bowl by the time you wish to serve it, stand in hot water for a few seconds to loosen it, then lift it off.

INGREDIENTS
125 g/4½ oz amaretti biscuits
2 tbsp cherry brandy
300 g/10½ oz fresh raspberries
50 g/1¾ oz caster sugar
300 ml/10 fl oz double cream
150 ml/5 fl oz single cream
3 tbsp cocoa powder
2 tbsp icing sugar

The redcurrant sprigs suggested for decorating can be frozen so that you have them when you are ready to serve the ice cream. Freeze the whole sprigs and they keep their shape.

Iced Redcurrant & Mascarpone Terrine

INGREDIENTS

225 g/8 oz fresh redcurrants, plus
    extra sprigs to decorate
finely grated rind and juice of
    1 large orange
2 tbsp icing sugar
250 g/9 oz mascarpone cheese
150 ml/5 fl oz whipping cream

SERVES 6

Line a 450-g/1-lb loaf tin or 850-ml/1½-pint oblong freezerproof plastic container with greaseproof paper, allowing it to hang over the edges of the container so that the ice cream can be easily removed. Strip the redcurrants from their stalks using the prongs of a fork and put in a bowl. Using the back of a wooden spoon, crush the redcurrants.

Add the orange rind and juice to the redcurrants and mix together. Sift in the icing sugar, then mix well. Add the mascarpone and mix until well blended. Whip the cream until it holds its shape. Add to the redcurrant mixture and fold in until well blended.

Turn the mixture into the prepared tin or plastic container, smooth the surface and freeze, uncovered, for 4 hours, or until firm or required. Cover the container with a lid for storing.

To serve the ice cream, uncover, stand the tin or plastic container in hot water for a few seconds to loosen it, then invert it on to a serving dish. Remove the greaseproof paper and, using a hot knife, cut the terrine into slices. Serve decorated with redcurrant sprigs.

Nesselrode is the name given to a selection of dishes, all of which contain chestnut purée. It is named after a nineteenth-century Russian diplomat, and is an ideal dessert to serve at Christmas.

Nesselrode Bombe

INGREDIENTS
175 g/6 oz mixed dried fruit
4 tbsp cherry brandy
300 ml/10 fl oz single cream
1 vanilla pod
4 egg yolks
85 g/3 oz caster sugar
250 g/9 oz canned peeled chestnuts
300 ml/10 fl oz double cream
50 g/1¾ oz glacé cherries, chopped

SERVES 8

Put the dried fruit in a bowl, add the kirsch or brandy and stir together. Leave to soak for 2–3 hours, stirring occasionally, until the liquid is absorbed. Meanwhile, pour the single cream into a heavy-based saucepan, add the vanilla pod and bring almost to the boil. Remove from the heat and leave to infuse for 15 minutes.

Put the egg yolks and sugar in a large bowl and whisk together until pale and the mixture leaves a trail when the whisk is lifted. Remove the vanilla pod from the cream, then slowly add the cream to the egg mixture, stirring all the time with a wooden spoon.

Strain the mixture into the rinsed-out saucepan or a double boiler and cook over a low heat for 10–15 minutes, stirring all the time, until the mixture thickens enough to coat the back of the spoon. Do not allow the mixture to boil or it will curdle. Remove the custard from the heat and leave to cool for at least 1 hour, stirring from time to time to prevent a skin from forming.

Put the chestnuts in a food processor or blender and process to form a purée. Whip the double cream until it just holds its shape. Fold in the soaked fruits and the cherries until well blended.

When the custard is cold, add the chestnut purée and whisk together. Fold in the cream and fruit mixture, then pour into a 1.4-litre/2½-pint pudding bowl, cover and freeze for 5 hours, or until firm or required.

Take the ice cream out of the freezer about 30 minutes before you are ready to serve it. Uncover, place a serving plate over the bowl, invert it and leave at room temperature. If it is not possible to remove the bowl by the time you wish to serve it, stand it in hot water for a few seconds to loosen it, then lift it off.

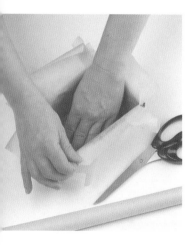

Chocolate and ice cream have to be one of the most delicious dessert combinations of all. This makes an ideal dinner-party dessert as it can be prepared ahead.

Chocolate Peppermint Crisp Terrine

INGREDIENTS
300 ml/10 fl oz single cream
½ tsp peppermint essence
4 egg yolks
115 g/4 oz caster sugar
200 g/7 oz plain dark chocolate
    peppermint crisps
300 ml/10 fl oz double cream
chocolate leaves, to decorate

SERVES 6–8

Line a 450-g/1-lb loaf tin or 850-ml/1½-pint oblong freezerproof plastic container with greaseproof paper, allowing it to hang over the edges of the container so that the ice cream can be easily removed. Pour the single cream into a heavy-based saucepan and bring almost to the boil. Remove from the heat and stir in the peppermint essence.

Put the egg yolks and sugar in a large bowl and whisk together until pale and the mixture leaves a trail when the whisk is lifted. Slowly add the cream, stirring all the time with a wooden spoon.

Strain the mixture into the rinsed-out saucepan or a double boiler and cook over a low heat for 10–15 minutes, stirring all the time, until the mixture thickens enough to coat the back of the spoon. Do not allow the mixture to boil or it will curdle. Remove the custard from the heat and leave to cool for at least 1 hour, stirring from time to time to prevent a skin from forming.

Meanwhile, put the peppermint crisps, a few at a time, into a food processor and chop into small pieces. Alternatively, chop the peppermint crisps into small pieces by hand.

Whip the double cream until it just holds its shape. When the custard is cold, stir in the peppermint crisp pieces, then fold in the whipped cream until well blended.

Turn the mixture into the prepared tin or plastic container and then freeze, uncovered, for 4 hours, or until firm or required. Cover the container with a lid for storing.

To serve the ice cream, uncover, stand the tin or plastic container in hot water for a few seconds to loosen it, then invert it on to a serving dish. Remove the greaseproof paper and, using a hot knife, cut the terrine into slices. Serve decorated with the chocolate leaves.

index